Bible
Word Search
Collection #8

BARBOUR
PUBLISHING, INC.
Uhrichsville, Ohio

© MCMXCVII by Barbour Publishing, Inc.

ISBN 1-57748-102-X

All Scripture references are from the Authorized King James Version of the Bible.

Published by Barbour Publishing, Inc.
P.O. Box 719
Uhrichsville, Ohio 44683
http://www.barbourbooks.com

ecpa Member of the
Evangelical Christian
Publishers Association

Printed in the United States of America.

Bible
Word Search
Collection #8

1

Kathleen Tailer

ISRAELITE PRIESTS

AARON	JUDGE
AHIMAAZ	KINGS
AHITUB	LAW
AMARIAH	LEADER
AZARIAH	LEVITICUS
CHRONICLES	MESSAGE
ELEAZAR	NUMBERS
EXODUS	PHINEHAS
EZRA	SAMUEL
FAITHFUL	SERAIAH
GOD	TABERNACLE
HIGH	TEMPLE
HILKIAH	WORSHIPER
INSTRUCTIONS	ZADOK

```
Z A I A E L C A N R E B A T L
A H N H H A S E R A I A H G N
D I S T I Z F A I T H M P O O
O T T M L A T E M P L O L D R
K U R A K R L A W S I K U S A
O B U A I I G E F R S J F E A
S U C Z A A H H R E A U H L S
U Q T C H H G A X B M D T C A
C Z I T T I Z O S M U G I I H
I A O I H A D G A U E E A N E
T A N O E U N R O N L A F O N
I M S L S I Z L E A D E R R I
V I E W K E T E M P L E A H H
E H W O R S H I P E R C B C P
L A M A R I A H M E S S A G E
```

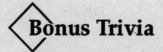

Bonus Trivia

What is the rest of the proverb, "My son, if sinners entice thee—"?

"Consent thou not," Proverbs 1:10.

5

2

Kathleen Tailer

MOTHERS IN THE BIBLE

AHINOAM

ATHALIAH

AZUBAH

BATHSHEBA

BILHAH

EUNICE

EVE

HAGGITH

HANNAH

HEPHZIBAH

HERODIAS

JEDIDAH

JEHOADDAN

JERUSHA

JOCHEBED

LEAH

MAACAH

MARY

MESHULLEMETH

NAOMI

RACHEL

RAHAB

REBEKAH

RUTH

SALOME

SARAH

TAMAR

VASHTI

ZEBUDAH

ZILPAH

```
I  B  A  H  A  R  Z  E  B  U  D  A  H  S  H
T  S  H  L  Z  T  J  E  R  U  S  H  A  Z  J
H  A  K  M  U  L  I  M  O  A  N  L  B  A  E
S  T  H  O  B  I  A  H  I  N  O  A  M  L  H
A  H  E  T  A  J  E  D  I  D  A  H  N  E  O
V  A  P  M  H  Z  O  R  A  C  H  E  L  A  A
S  L  H  J  E  R  S  O  B  I  L  H  A  H  D
N  I  Z  A  E  L  A  V  E  V  E  V  T  H  D
H  A  I  H  H  M  L  E  H  A  N  N  A  H  A
A  H  B  I  A  A  O  U  S  N  J  R  M  T  N
K  M  A  N  G  A  M  N  H  S  A  U  A  O  Y
E  T  H  O  G  C  E  I  T  S  J  T  R  R  A
B  K  H  A  I  A  H  C  A  V  E  H  A  K  M
E  I  A  M  T  H  L  E  B  K  T  M  O  S  I
R  J  O  C  H  E  B  E  D  Z  I  L  P  A  H
```

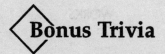

Bonus Trivia

Whose is the saying about the axe laid to the root of the trees?

John the Baptist's. Matthew 3:10.

3

Kathleen Tailer

PRAISE IN PSALMS

ADMIRATION	JUST
APPRECIATION	KINGDOM
BLESSINGS	LIGHT
CELEBRATE	LOVE
CREATION	LOVING
DAVID	MAJESTY
DELIVERER	MUSIC
EXALT	PATIENT
FAITHFUL	PRAISE
FORGIVENESS	PRAYERS
GLORIOUS	ROCK
GLORY	SHARED
HEARTFELT	SING
HOPE	THANKS
JOY	WORKS

```
W F L F O R G I V E N E S S L
O A M A J E S T Y H K A C G O
R I A G L O R I O U S T R N T
K T Q P L O V I N G I M E I H
S H R S P E X A L T N U A S A
N F U T C R D L H W G S T S N
O U P P V E E A I O X I I E K
I L A R L K L C V G P C O L S
T G T A A O I E I I H E N B T
A L I I J Y V N B A D T Y J D
R O E S U B E E G R T Z A O E
I R N E S O R R N D A I B Y R
M Y T N T N E I S E O T O T A
D B S T A E R C O P S M E N H
A R O C K H E A R T F E L T S
```

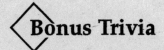

Bonus Trivia

Who said of the religious leaders of his day
that they said "Peace, peace," when there
was no peace?

Jeremiah. Jeremiah 6:14.

4
ISRAELITE FEASTS
IN LEVITICUS

Kathleen Tailer

ATONEMENT	LORD
COMMITMENT	PASSOVER
CROPS	PROTECTION
DELIVERANCE	PROTECTION
DESERT	RESTORATION
EGYPT	SEVEN
EXODUS	SLAVERY
FELLOWSHIP	TABERNACLES
FIRSTFRUITS	THANKSGIVING
GOD	TRUMPETS
GUIDANCE	TRUST
JOY	UNLEAVENED BREAD
LEVITICUS	WEEKS

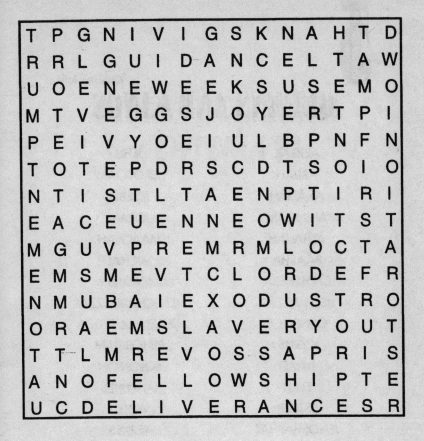

```
T P G N I V I G S K N A H T D
R R L G U I D A N C E L T A W
U O E N E W E E K S U S E M O
M T V E G G S J O Y E R T P I
P E I V Y O E I U L B P N F N
T O T E P D R S C D T S O I O
N T I S T L T A E N P T I R I
E A C E U E N N E O W I T S T
M G U V P R E M R M L O C T A
E M S M E V T C L O R D E F R
N M U B A I E X O D U S T R O
O R A E M S L A V E R Y O U T
T T L M R E V O S S A P R I S
A N O F E L L O W S H I P T E
U C D E L I V E R A N C E S R
```

◇ **Bonus Trivia**

What did Paul call "the first commandment with promise"?

"Honour thy father and mother." Ephesians 6:2.

5
Kathleen Tailer

QUEENS AND KINGS

ABIGAIL	JEHU
ABIJAH	JEROBOAM
AHAZIAH	JEZEBEL
AHINOAM	JORAM
ATHALIAH	MAACHAH
BAASHA	MICHAL
BATHSHEBA	NADAB
BELSHAZZAR	NEBUCHADNEZZAR
CANDACE	QUEEN OF SHEBA
CYRUS	REHOBOAM
DAVID	SOLOMON
ELAH	TAHPENES
ESTHER	VASHTI
JEHOSHAPHAT	XERXES

```
A M J E H O S H A P H A T T R
B A T H S H E B A X E R X A E
I A H A I L A H T A H A Z H H
J C K B C Y R U S N T Z A P O
A H J A M I C H A L E Z H E B
H A O A T J T L P N C A I N O
J H R S Z S E M D O A H N E A
D O A H E B A A H M D S O S M
A U M A E O H A E O N L A Z I
V H N Z B C I S E L A E M B T
I E E O U Z E Q H O C B E A H
D J R B A X U L T S H O L D S
T E E H R A B I G A I L A A A
J N A E S T H E R K T P H N V
Q U X A B E H S F O N E E U Q
```

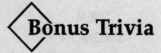

Bonus Trivia

Who asked God to put his tears into His
bottle?

David. Psalms 56:8.

6

Kathleen Tailer

FATHERS

AARON	JOB
ABRAHAM	JONATHAN
ADAM	JOSEPH
AHAB	JUDAH
ALPHAEUS	KISH
BENJAMIN	LABAN
DAN	LEVI
DAVID	MORDECAI
ELI	MOSES
ELKANAH	NAPHTALI
ENOCH	NOAH
GAD	REUBEN
HAM	SAMUEL
ISAAC	SAUL
JACOB	SETH
JAPHETH	SHEM
JEPHTHAH	SOLOMON
JETHRO	

```
T K O J E P H T H A H L E V I
J B M E L K A N A H N D A N L
A S A O I S A A C O T B B I J
P L E L R J D I V A D E R L O
H O U O P D K N O A H N A A S
E L T A R H E I J O B J H T E
T A J E S H A C S K E A A H P
H B O C S S T E A H L M M P H
L A N N A O E E U I I I A A C
B N A E M L M T J S M N M N O
O A T B U O A P H J E N O C H
C A H U E M H N O U H L S H T
A R A E L O A O I D S I E A G
J O N R J N B T C A B C S M A
K N J O N A T H A H A D A M D
```

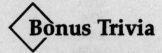

Bonus Trivia

Who laid his sin to "the woman whom thou gavest to be with me"?

Adam. Genesis 3:12.

7

Helen Weeks

ANIMALS & BIRDS OF THE BIBLE

ADDER
ANT
ANTELOPE
APE
ASP
ASS
BADGER
BAT
BEAR
BEE
BEETLE
BULLOCK
CAMEL
COCKATRICE
COLT
DROMEDARY
EAGLE
EWE
FLEA
FOX
FROG
GAZELLE
GNAT
GOAT
GRASSHOPPER

HARE
HART
HAWK
HEIFER
HORNET
HORSE
KID
KINE
LAMB
LICE
LION
LOCUST
MOLE
MOTH
MOUSE
OWL
OX
RAM
RAVEN
SNAIL
SPARROW
STORK
SWINE
VULTURE

A	R	A	E	B	T	C	A	E	L	L	E	Z	A	G
N	D	D	I	K	A	N	N	L	A	Z	C	K	H	E
T	H	D	B	M	B	D	A	T	U	G	I	I	O	L
E	A	P	E	H	E	W	G	E	B	N	L	N	R	O
L	W	L	A	R	R	O	B	E	W	Z	E	E	S	M
O	K	S	O	L	A	S	E	B	R	G	F	V	E	T
P	S	A	A	T	H	V	U	L	T	U	R	E	A	Y
E	W	E	M	R	E	L	E	T	A	B	O	N	U	R
J	L	O	B	N	L	S	S	D	L	O	G	F	S	A
F	T	M	I	O	U	U	N	Y	X	O	F	H	T	D
H	A	W	C	O	C	K	A	T	R	I	C	E	O	E
L	S	K	M	O	W	J	I	T	H	F	N	I	R	M
I	P	E	L	R	C	L	L	R	K	R	A	F	K	O
O	S	P	A	R	R	O	W	A	O	G	P	E	S	R
N	Z	M	R	E	P	P	O	H	S	S	A	R	G	D

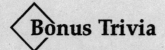

Bonus Trivia

Who said of God that He is "of purer eyes than to behold evil," and that He cannot look on iniquity?

Habakkuk. Habakkuk 1:13.

8

Helen Weeks

BOOKS OF THE NEW TESTAMENT

ACTS	MARK
COLOSSIANS	MATTHEW
CORINTHIANS	PETER
EPHESIANS	PHILEMON
GALATIANS	PHILIPPIANS
HEBREWS	REVELATION
JAMES	ROMANS
JOHN	THESSALONIANS
JUDE	TIMOTHY
LUKE	TITUS

```
T I M O T H Y Z S M E T S O G
P H I L E M O N U S W N N B A
I Z E J K B S E T M O R A N L
Y H D S T W O L I I B K I H A
M A F S S R M G T S P M S O T
S W C A N A J A E B G W E J I
N E Z T E A L M R L Y Z H K A
A H P M S E I O A K J C P S N
I T B J V S M P N E O I E M S
S T Y E M A E L P I F M L T B
S A R A N G U N S I A W S R Y
O M F S I K W S E J L N A E P
L A J U E D U J T M O I S T J
O K S W E R B E H K W G H E B
C O R I N T H I A N S C M P U
```

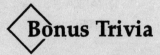

Bonus Trivia

Of whom did Christ say that they loved "the uppermost seats in the synagogues"?

The Pharisees. Luke 11:43.

19

9

Helen Weeks

CITIES, COUNTRIES, AND PLACES PAUL TRAVELED TO AND THROUGH

APPII FORUM	NEAPOLIS
ARABIA	PAMPHYLIA
ASIA	PAPHOS
CAESAREA	PHILIPPI
CHIOS	PHOENICIA
COOS	PISIDIA
DAMASCUS	SAMOS
GREECE	SELEUCIA
ITALY	SMYRNA
JUDEA	SYRIA
LYCAONIA	THESSALONICA
LYCIA	THREE TAVERNS
MACEDONIA	THYATIRA
MELITA	TYRE
MILETUS	

```
N E A P O L I S B S S A A M P
C P F A G W O Z Y U O I I D I
A H N E Y H I R A T I S N A S
I O K R P S I P R E H A O M I
B E U A S A Z M P L C P A A D
A N P S I A U D S I H P C S I
R I A E T N M T N M L I Y C A
A C N A A I O O K F Y I L U I
R I R C L I L D S O C F H S L
I A Y V Y A C R E V I O G P Y
T P M B S I K U N C A R R S H
A B S S L E W J E H A U E S P
Y V E U K R A T I L E M E O M
H H W M P Y S J U D E A C O A
T H R E E T A V E R N S E C P
```

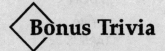

Bonus Trivia

What is the proverb about spreading a net in the sight of a bird?

"Surely in vain the net is spread in the sight of any bird." Proverbs 1:17.

10

Helen Weeks

CITIES, COUNTRIES, AND PLACES PAUL TRAVELED TO AND THROUGH: PART TWO

ACHAIA	GALATIA
AMPHIPOLIS	ICONIUM
ANTIOCH	JERUSALEM
APOLLONIA	LASEA
ASSOS	LYSTRA
ATHENS	MYRA
ATTALIA	PATARA
BEREA	PERGA
CENCHREA	PHRYGIA
CILICIA	RHODES
CNIDUS	ROME
CORINTH	SAMOTHRACIA
CRETE	SIDON
CYPRUS	SYRIA
DERBE	TARSUS
EPHESUS	TROAS
FAIR HAVENS	

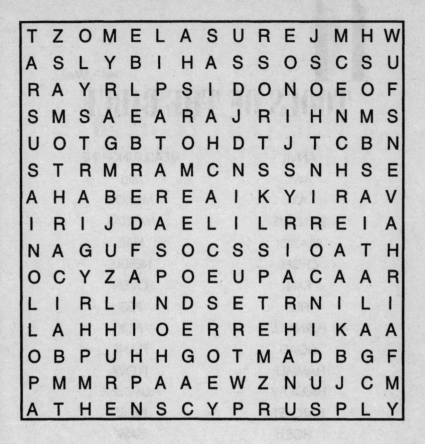

```
T Z O M E L A S U R E J M H W
A S L Y B I H A S S O S C S U
R A Y R L P S I D O N O E O F
S M S A E A R A J R I H N M S
U O T G B T O H D T J T C B N
S T R M R A M C N S S N H S E
A H A B E R E A I K Y I R A V
I R I J D A E L I L R R E I A
N A G U F S O C S S I O A T H
O C Y Z A P O E U P A C A A R
L I R L I N D S E T R N I L I
L A H H I O E R R E H I K A A
O B P U H H G O T M A D B G F
P M M R P A A E W Z N U J C M
A T H E N S C Y P R U S P L Y
```

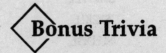

Bonus Trivia

To whom did God say, "The Lord searcheth all hearts"?

Solomon. 1 Chronicles 28:9.

11

Helen Weeks

TOOLS OF THE BIBLE

ANVIL	MEASURING LINE
AWL	MILL
AX	MIRROR
BELLOWS	MORTAR
BRAZIER	NAIL
CHISEL	NEEDLE
FAN	OVEN
FILE	PEG
FURNACE	PICK
GOAD	PLANE
HAMMER	PLOW
HARROW	PLUMBLINE
HATCHET	PRESS
HOE	SAW
KNIFE	SHOVEL
LEVEL	SICKLE
MALLET	SLEDGE
MARKING TOOLS	TONGS
MATTOCK	WHEEL
MAUL	YOKE

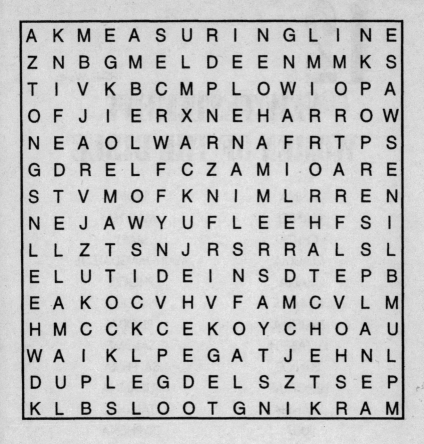

```
A K M E A S U R I N G L I N E
Z N B G M E L D E E N M M K S
T I V K B C M P L O W I O P A
O F J I E R X N E H A R R O W
N E A O L W A R N A F R T P S
G D R E L F C Z A M I O A R E
S T V M O F K N I M L R R E N
N E J A W Y U F L E E H F S I
L L Z T S N J R S R R A L S L
E L U T I D E I N S D T E P B
E A K O C V H V F A M C V L M
H M C C K E K O Y C H O A U
W A I K L P E G A T J E H N L
D U P L E G D E L S Z T S E P
K L B S L O O T G N I K R A M
```

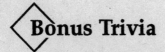

Bonus Trivia

Who said, "Behold the handmaid of the Lord; be it unto me according to thy word"?

The Virgin Mary. Luke 1:38.

12

Helen Weeks

NEW TESTAMENT WOMEN OF THE BIBLE

ANNA

BERNICE

CHLOE

CLAUDIA

DIANA

DORCAS

DRUSILLA

ELIZABETH

EUNICE

HERODIAS

JOANNA

JULIA

LOIS

LYDIA

MARTHA

MARY

MARY MAGDALENE

PHOEBE

PRISCILLA

RHODA

SALOME

SAPPHIRA

SUSANNA

TABITHA

TRYPHENA

```
R F A W L B A A N E H P Y R T
H E R O D I A S P E Z E M C E
E M O L A S E R C B B A A A L
S I O L A K I I E E E N H D I
F W Z C H S N R O A U N T O Z
A U R S C U N H M S D A I H A
I O K I E I P A T W O S B R B
D C L M C H L O E Z I U A C E
U L S E A R I H P P A S T G T
A Y K T Z A L L I S U R D W H
L D J R M A H M A N N A O J E
C I U A W R A T G K N Y U B T
M A N S F R U L R A S L C R Z
E N R L Y F K M I A I Z M P O
A Z E N E L A D G A M Y R A M
```

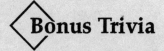

Bonus Trivia

Finish Paul's saying, "The natural man receiveth not—"?

"The things of the Spirit of God."
1 Corinthians 2:14.

27

13

Helen Weeks

KINGS FROM THE BIBLE

ABIJAH	JEHOASH
ABIMELECH	JEHOIACHIN
AHAB	JEHOSHAPHAT
AHAZ	JEHU
AHAZIAH	JOASH
AMAZIAH	JOSIAH
AMON	NADAB
ARTAXERXES	OMRI
ASA	PEKAH
AZARIAH	REHOBOAM
DARIUS	SAUL
DAVID	SHALLUM
ELAH	SOLOMON
HEZEKIAH	ZECHARIAH
HOSEA	ZEDEKIAH
JEHOAHAZ	ZIMRI

```
A Z A R I A H H A I K E Z E H
H H M E J A B I J A H M N N Z
A A U Z H B Z E B A A T O A E
Z I F A N I R L K O J H M D C
I K L C M M G E B O T I A A H
A E A R S E P O A A M E S B A
H D I K U L H S H A L H S I R
Z E A H U E H P O Z A U R G I
A Z E A R C A B K L I M A Z A
H J S I M H O M L R O G E R H
A N O S S R E U A B A M C L D
O G H O E Z M D P Z O A O I U
H C H J E H O A S H I S V N F
E E S E X R E X A T R A H A Z
J E H O I A C H I N D E H K M
```

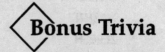

Bonus Trivia

What is the first part of the sentence which ends, "and into his courts with praise"?

"Enter into his gates with thanksgiving."
Psalms 100:4.

29

14

Helen Weeks

OLD TESTAMENT
WOMEN OF THE BIBLE

ABIGAIL	JOCHEBED
ABISHAG	KETURAH
ADAH	LEAH
BATHSHEBA	MICHAL
BILHAH	MIRIAM
DEBORAH	ORPAH
DELILAH	PENINNAH
DINAH	RACHEL
ESTHER	RAHAB
EVE	REBEKAH
GOMER	RUTH
HAGAR	SARAH
HANNAH	TAMAR
HEPHZIBAH	VASHTI
HULDAH	ZERESH
JAEL	ZIPPORAH
JEZEBEL	

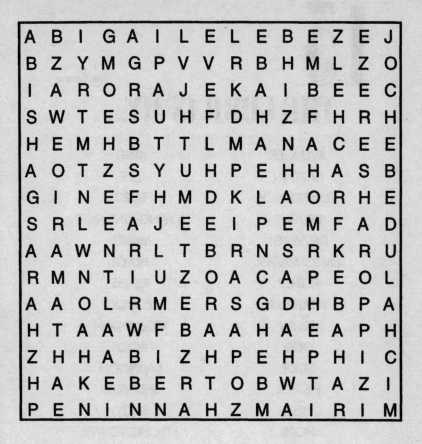

```
A B I G A I L E L E B E Z E J
B Z Y M G P V V R B H M L Z O
I A R O R A J E K A I B E E C
S W T E S U H F D H Z F H R H
H E M H B T T L M A N A C E E
A O T Z S Y U H P E H H A S B
G I N E F H M D K L A O R H E
S R L E A J E E I P E M F A D
A A W N R L T B R N S R K R U
R M N T I U Z O A C A P E O L
A A O L R M E R S G D H B P A
H T A A W F B A A H A E A P H
Z H H A B I Z H P E H P H I C
H A K E B E R T O B W T A Z I
P E N I N N A H Z M A I R I M
```

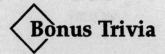

Bonus Trivia

Of whom was it asked in astonishment
whether he also was among the prophets?

Saul. 1 Samuel 10:11,12.

15

Joe Saxton

THE LORD IS MY. . .

AVENGER	KING
CAPTAIN	LIFE
CONFIDENCE	LORD
DELIGHT	LOVING KINDNESS
DELIVERER	MAKER
ENCOURAGER	PEACE
FATHER	PRAISE
FORTRESS	PROVIDER
GLORY	REDEMPTION
GOD	ROCK
GUIDE	SALVATION
HEALER	SHEPHERD
HELP	SHIELD
HOPE	STRONG TOWER
INHERITANCE	TEACHER
JOY	VICTORY
JUDGE	

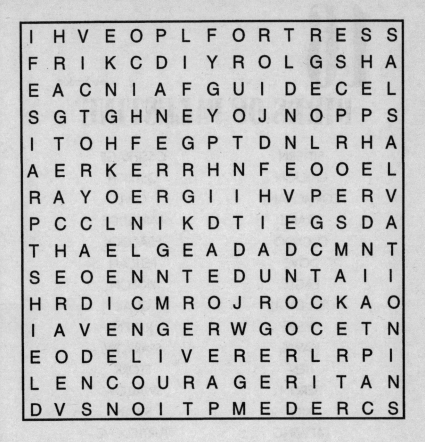

```
I H V E O P L F O R T R E S S
F R I K C D I Y R O L G S H A
E A C N I A F G U I D E C E L
S G T G H N E Y O J N O P P S
I T O H F E G P T D N L R H A
A E R K E R R H N F E O O E L
R A Y O E R G I I H V P E R V
P C C L N I K D T I E G S D A
T H A E L G E A D A D C M N T
S E O E N N T E D U N T A I I
H R D I C M R O J R O C K A O
I A V E N G E R W G O C E T N
E O D E L I V E R E R L R P I
L E N C O U R A G E R I T A N
D V S N O I T P M E D E R C S
```

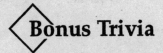

Bonus Trivia

Of whom did the Lord ask, "Who is this that darkeneth counsel by words without knowledge?"

Job. Job 38:2.

16

Joe Saxton

BIRDS OF PALESTINE

BITTERN

CHICKEN

CORMORANT

CRANE

CUCKOO

DOVE

EAGLE

GIER EAGLE

GLEDE

HAWK

HEN

HERON

KITE

LAPWING

NIGHTHAWK

OSPREY

OSSIFRAGE

OSTRICH

OWL

PARTRIDGE

PEACOCK

PELICAN

PIGEON

QUAIL

RAVEN

SPARROW

STORK

SWALLOW

SWAN

TURTLEDOVE

VULTURE

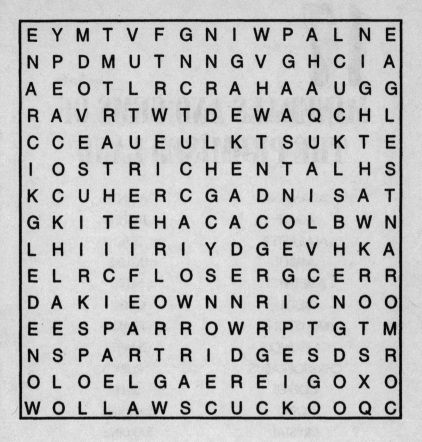

```
E Y M T V F G N I W P A L N E
N P D M U T N N G V G H C I A
A E O T L R C R A H A A U G G
R A V R T W T D E W A Q C H L
C C E A U E U L K T S U K T E
I O S T R I C H E N T A L H S
K C U H E R C G A D N I S A T
G K I T E H A C A C O L B W N
L H I I I R I Y D G E V H K A
E L R C F L O S E R G C E R R
D A K I E O W N N R I C N O O
E E S P A R R O W R P T G T M
N S P A R T R I D G E S D S R
O L O E L G A E R E I G O X O
W O L L A W S C U C K O O Q C
```

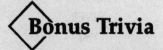

Bonus Trivia

Finish the quotation from Isaiah: "I will say
to the north, Give up; and to the south, Keep
not back."

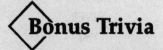

"Bring my sons from far, and my
daughters from the ends of the earth."
Isaiah 43:6.

17

Joe Saxton

MINERALS AND GEMS OF THE PROMISED LAND

ADAMANT	JACINTH
AGATE	JASPER
ALABASTER	LEAD
AMBER	LIGURE
AMETHYST	NITRE
BERYL	ONYX
BRIMSTONE	PEARL
CARBUNCLE	QUARTZ
CHRYSOPRASUS	RUBY
COPPER	SALT
CORAL	SAPPHIRE
CRYSTAL	SARDINE
DIAMOND	SARDONYX
EMERALD	SILVER
FLINT	TIN
GOLD	TOPAZ
IRON	

```
Z S L E A D Z A P O T G S U L
T A L O S I J A C I N T H A N
R P A N U A R G L I G U R E R
A P Y L S L S O D D L O G U C
U H X P A F L I N T C R B A C
Q I E W R B A L L N U Y A T O
B R E T P M A G O V I K E E P
R E N O O T M S A B E T L X P
I D I N S T E E T T E R C Y E
M Y D Y Y D T V O E E E N N R
S X R F R E H N G O R L U O F
T C A P H Q Y R R T T E B D R
O R S R C X S J I C A L R R N
N R E B M A T N A M A D A A L
E M E R A L D L Y R E B C S B
```

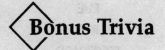

Bonus Trivia

What is Christ's question about spoiled salt?

"If the salt have lost his saltness,
wherewith will ye season it?" Mark 9:50.

37

18

Joe Saxton

BIBLICAL GRAINS, VEGETABLES, AND SEASONINGS

ALOE	GOURDS
ANISE	HYSSOP
BALSAM	LEEKS
BAY TREE	LENTILS
BDELLIUM	MALLOW
BEANS	MANDRAKES
CALAMUS	MILLET
CAMPHIRE	MUSTARD
CASSIA	MYRRH
CINNAMON	MYRTLE
CORIANDER	ONIONS
CORN	RUE
CUCUMBER	RYE
FRANKINCENSE	SPIKENARD
GALL	STACTE
GARLIC	WHEAT

```
H D M A N D R A K E S T N H T
P W L S H L B E R G E O R A R
E O C A L A M U S L M R E A C
E L J A L I L C L A Y H M E F
R L G S T R T I N M W U E R C
T A A H P A M N I X I E A I U
Y M W Y S I I D E L R N L H C
A I S S A C K S L L K Y O P U
B O K S N E T E D I R U E M M
A O E O P A D F N R A L O A B
R N E P A B E C B A U I F C E
C I L R A G E B Q N R O C O R
C O R I A N D E R I B D G V S
S N M U S T A R D S T A C T E
G S A E E R O N O E L T R Y M
```

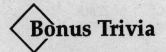

Bonus Trivia

Finish the quotation, "In that he himself hath suffered being tempted—."

"He is able to succour them that are tempted." Hebrew 2:18.

19

Joe Saxton

OLD TESTAMENT PAGAN DEITIES

ADRAMMELECH	ISHTAR
AMON	ISIS
AMON-RA	MARDUK
ASHERAH	MENI
ASHTOROTH	MERODACH
BAAL	MILCOM
BEL	MOLECH
BELIAL	NEBO
BERITH	NERGAL
CHEMOSH	PEOR
CHIUN	RIMMON
DAGON	SIKKUTH
EL	TERAPHIM
GAD	ZEBUL

```
S A G Z I N E M I L C O M R L
I I D A R P H A R E H S A E A
K A S S D O G O N E J S M M A
K F A I C H E M O S H S L E B
U W K S L R M P L T C Z C R C
T R K U D R A M O L E C H O T
H A A M O N T R J L C I D I
E T R D N I O S I D E O U A M
A H I D A T N B L M M K N C M
I S G R H N E R E A M Z J H U
Z I T W E L O R R C A O D R T
E D L R I B A N P T R G N M Z
B S G A E E O U A I D A G O N
U A L N I M H A Z O A N G O G
L C M D A T E R A P H I M M Z
```

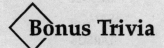

◇ Bonus Trivia

What is the rest of the verse in Deuteronomy beginning, "If from thence thou shalt seek the Lord thy God—"?

Deuteronomy 4:29.
all thy heart and with all thy soul."
"Thou shalt find him, if thou seek him with

41

20

Joe Saxton

PAUL'S THIRD MISSIONARY JOURNEY: CITIES, REGIONS, NATIONS

ACHAIA	JERUSALEM
ALEXANDRIA	LYSTRA
ANTIOCH	MACEDONIA
ASIA	MILETUS
ASSOS	MITYLENE
ATHENS	NEAPOLIS
BEREA	PATARA
CAESAREA	PHILIPPI
CHIOS	PHRYGIA
COOS	PTOLEMAIS
CYPRUS	RHODES
DERBE	SAMOS
EPHESUS	TARSUS
GALATIA	TROAS
ICONIUM	TYRE

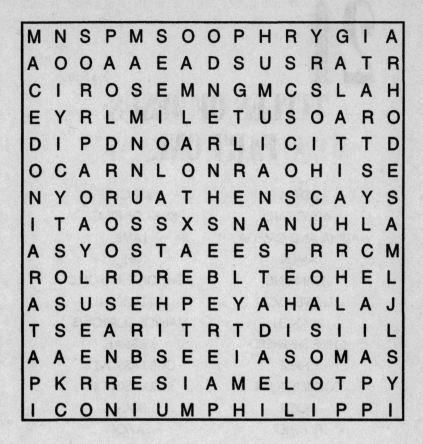

```
M N S P M S O O P H R Y G I A
A O O A A E A D S U S R A T R
C I R O S E M N G M C S L A H
E Y R L M I L E T U S O A R O
D I P D N O A R L I C I T T D
O C A R N L O N R A O H I S E
N Y O R U A T H E N S C A Y S
I T A O S S X S N A N U H L A
A S Y O S T A E E S P R R C M
R O L R D R E B L T E O H E L
A S U S E H P E Y A H A L A J
T S E A R I T R T D I S I I L
A A E N B S E E I A S O M A S
P K R R E S I A M E L O T P Y
I C O N I U M P H I L I P P I
```

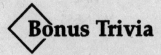

Bonus Trivia

What saying of Christ's concerning His pre-existence introduces Abraham?

"Before Abraham was, I am." John 8:58.

21

Joe Saxton

TITLES OF JESUS:
PART ONE

ADAM	JUST ONE
ADVOCATE	KING OF KINGS
ALPHA AND OMEGA	LAMB
AMEN	LIFE
BEGINNING	LIGHT OF THE WORLD
BELOVED SON	LORD OF ALL
BRANCH	MAN OF SORROWS
CHIEF SHEPHERD	MESSIAH
CHRIST	OUR PASSOVER
CORNERSTONE	RESURRECTION
DOOR	ROCK
FINISHER	SAVIOR
HOLY ONE	VINE
I AM	WITNESS
IMMANUEL	

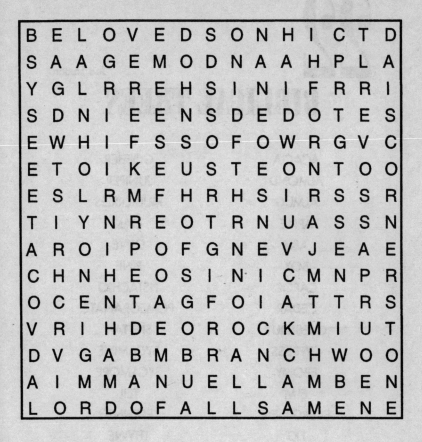

```
B E L O V E D S O N H I C T D
S A A G E M O D N A A H P L A
Y G L R R E H S I N I F R R I
S D N I E E N S D E D O T E S
E W H I F S S O F O W R G V C
E T O I K E U S T E O N T O O
E S L R M F H R H S I R S S R
T I Y N R E O T R N U A S S N
A R O I P O F G N E V J E A E
C H N H E O S I N I C M N P R
O C E N T A G F O I A T T R S
V R I H D E O R O C K M I U T
D V G A B M B R A N C H W O O
A I M M A N U E L L A M B E N
L O R D O F A L L S A M E N E
```

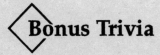

Bonus Trivia

What is Paul's saying about "respect of persons"?

"There is no respect of persons with God."
Romans 2:11.

45

22

Joe Saxton

BIBLICAL TREES

ACACIA	GOPHER
ALMOND	JUNIPER
ALMUG	MULBERRIES
APPLE	OAK
ASH	OLIVE
BOX	PINE
CAROB	PISTACHIO
CEDAR	POMEGRANATE
CHESTNUT	SHITTAH
CYPRESS	SYCAMINE
EBONY	SYCAMORE
ELM	TEIL
EVERGREEN	TEREBINTH
FIG	THYINE
FIR	

A	E	N	I	P	A	H	E	I	Y	D	B	E	L	M
G	C	Y	P	R	E	S	S	D	N	O	P	N	G	W
P	R	A	O	S	T	A	I	O	X	J	O	U	E	N
T	I	C	C	A	T	C	M	T	L	I	M	T	C	E
O	F	D	O	I	K	L	T	F	H	L	E	Y	C	E
S	H	I	T	T	A	H	I	C	A	I	G	U	H	R
E	H	G	U	E	Z	G	A	C	L	H	R	I	E	G
I	S	T	T	M	S	T	E	L	P	P	A	G	S	R
R	A	S	N	C	S	Y	L	U	B	L	N	O	T	E
R	A	E	N	I	M	A	C	Y	S	U	A	P	N	V
E	A	D	P	E	B	O	C	A	N	L	T	H	U	E
B	H	E	E	G	C	E	L	A	M	O	E	E	T	A
L	U	Q	I	C	G	T	R	I	R	O	B	R	Q	S
U	R	E	P	I	N	U	J	E	V	O	R	E	C	G
M	K	D	I	E	N	I	Y	H	T	E	B	E	M	A

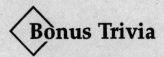

Bonus Trivia

What is the proverb about pride and a fall?

"Pride goeth before destruction, and an haughty spirit before a fall." Proverbs 16:18.

23

Joe Saxton

SATANIC SYNONYMS

ABADDON	FATHER OF LIES
ACCUSER	GOD OF THIS AGE
ADVERSARY	LIAR
ANGEL OF LIGHT	LUCIFER
ANOINTED CHERUB	MURDERER
APOLLYON	ROARING LION
BEELZEBUB	RULER OF DARKNESS
BELIAL	SATAN
DECEIVER	SERPENT
DEVIL	STRONG MAN
DRAGON	TEMPTER
ENEMY	THIEF
EVIL ONE	WICKED ONE

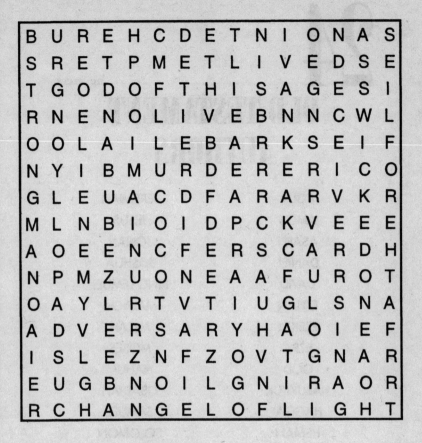

```
B U R E H C D E T N I O N A S
S R E T P M E T L I V E D S E
T G O D O F T H I S A G E S I
R N E N O L I V E B N N C W L
O O L A I L E B A R K S E I F
N Y I B M U R D E R E R I C O
G L E U A C D F A R A R V K R
M L N B I O I D P C K V E E E
A O E E N C F E R S C A R D H
N P M Z U O N E A A F U R O T
O A Y L R T V T I U G L S N A
A D V E R S A R Y H A O I E F
I S L E Z N F Z O V T G N A R
E U G B N O I L G N I R A O R
R C H A N G E L O F L I G H T
```

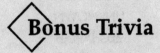

Bonus Trivia

Finish the promise in Leviticus, "Ye shall lie down—."

49

24

OLD TESTAMENT AUTHORS

Joe Saxton

AGUR	JEREMIAH
AMOS	JESUS
ASAPH	JONAH
DANIEL	JOSHUA
DAVID	KING LEMUEL
ETHAN	MALACHI
EZEKIEL	MICAH
EZRA	MOSES
GOD	NAHUM
HABUKKUK	OBADIAH
HAGGAI	SAMUEL
HEMAN	SOLOMON
HOLY SPIRIT	SONS OF KORAH
HOSEA	UNKNOWN
ISAIAH	ZECHARIAH
JEDUTHUN	ZEPHANIAH

I	R	Y	H	A	I	N	A	H	P	E	Z	D	I	O
C	H	I	S	C	R	D	O	M	U	H	A	N	B	N
N	S	A	S	B	I	O	L	L	S	N	R	A	O	R
U	P	R	I	H	A	G	G	A	I	U	D	M	E	P
H	M	Z	E	A	O	E	R	E	G	I	O	E	J	L
T	A	E	C	B	S	L	L	A	A	L	T	H	E	E
U	L	R	R	U	T	I	Y	H	O	H	O	U	R	U
D	A	I	O	K	L	E	W	S	A	S	M	E	E	M
E	C	U	N	K	N	O	W	N	P	A	P	Z	M	E
J	H	D	D	U	F	M	T	Y	S	I	M	E	I	L
D	I	A	V	K	A	O	I	L	G	U	R	K	A	G
A	R	H	E	A	O	M	S	C	C	H	S	I	H	N
V	A	U	H	S	O	J	O	N	A	H	W	E	T	I
I	G	O	M	M	O	S	E	S	O	H	A	L	J	K
D	H	A	I	R	A	H	C	E	Z	S	K	H	U	C

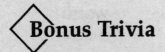

Bonus Trivia

In what book is the prayer, "Lead me to the rock that is higher than I"?

Psalms 61:2.

51

25

Joe Saxton

TITLES OF JESUS: PART TWO

ARM OF THE LORD	MORNING STAR
AUTHOR	PRINCE OF PEACE
BREAD OF LIFE	PROPHET
BUILDER	ROOT
CREATOR	SERVANT
FIRST	SHILOH
GOOD SHEPHERD	SON
HEAD	SON OF DAVID
HORN OF SALVATION	SON OF MAN
IMAGE OF GOD	STONE
JEHOVAH	SURETY
JUST	TRUTH
LAST	WAY
LEADER	WORD
LIGHT	

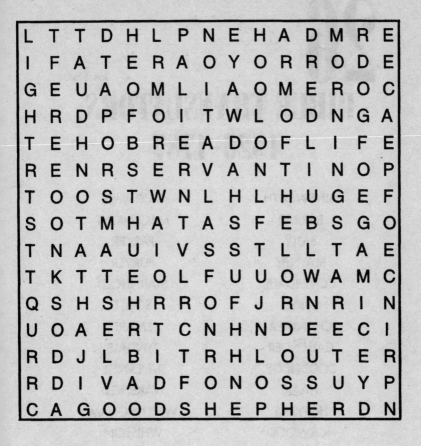

```
L T T D H L P N E H A D M R E
I F A T E R A O Y O R R O D E
G E U A O M L I A O M E R O C
H R D P F O I T W L O D N G A
T E H O B R E A D O F L I F E
R E N R S E R V A N T I N O P
T O O S T W N L H L H U G E F
S O T M H A T A S F E B S G O
T N A A U I V S S T L L T A E
T K T T E O L F U U O W A M C
Q S H S H R R O F J R N R I N
U O A E R T C N H N D E E C I
R D J L B I T R H L O U T E R
R D I V A D F O N O S S U Y P
C A G O O D S H E P H E R D N
```

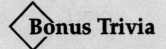

Bonus Trivia

Who said to a mighty king, "Let thy gifts be to thyself, and give thy rewards to another"?

Daniel to Belshazzar. Daniel 5:17

53

26
Joe Saxton

BIBLE TRANSLATORS:
1526–1787

AINSWORTH
BARBAR
BATLY
BLAYNEY
COVERDALE
CARYLL
CHANDLER
CALLENDER
DODDRIDGE
HAAK
HOPKINS
HORWOOD
JOYE
LEWIS
LOWTH

MORTIMER
MACKNIGHT
PARKER
PURVER
STARNHOLD
SCOTT
SMART
TYNDALE
TAVERNER
WAKEFIELD
WHITTINGHAM
WHISTON
WYNNE
WORSLEY

E	H	N	G	D	L	E	I	F	E	K	A	W	H	C
S	L	C	A	L	L	E	N	D	E	R	H	O	R	N
C	M	W	M	A	Y	M	E	O	N	I	R	R	E	G
T	C	A	D	A	R	A	T	Y	T	W	F	S	K	E
P	T	N	R	H	A	C	K	T	O	D	A	L	R	L
S	Y	O	W	T	C	K	I	O	M	J	Q	E	A	A
T	T	N	C	H	A	N	D	L	E	R	V	Y	P	D
A	R	A	T	S	G	I	K	I	E	R	T	T	I	R
V	Y	W	R	H	A	G	K	M	U	W	Y	N	N	E
E	H	L	A	N	L	H	I	P	L	E	W	I	S	V
R	T	M	T	Y	H	T	R	O	W	S	N	I	A	O
N	W	B	P	A	R	O	R	A	B	R	A	B	N	C
E	O	E	A	O	B	A	L	S	N	I	K	P	O	H
R	L	K	M	T	D	O	D	D	R	I	D	G	E	P
B	L	A	Y	N	E	Y	G	N	O	T	S	I	H	W

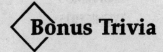

Bonus Trivia

To whom did the Lord say, "Speak unto the children of Israel, that they go forward"?

Moses. Exodus 14:15.

55

27

Joe Saxton

MEN IN "ACTS"ION:
PAUL'S PARTNERS

AGABUS	LUKE
ANANIAS	MANAEN
APOLLOS	MARK
AQUILA	MATTHIAS
ARISTARCHUS	PETER
BARNABAS	PHILIP
CORNELIUS	SECUNDUS
CRISPUS	SILAS
ERASTUS	SIMEON
GAIUS	SOPATER
JAMES	STEPHEN
JASON	TIMOTHY
JOHN	TROPHIMUS
LUCIUS	TYCHICHUS

S	S	E	C	U	N	D	U	S	V	N	H	W	O	S
G	U	U	O	M	D	P	I	T	U	G	O	K	E	E
O	T	S	M	J	A	N	R	E	T	I	R	S	S	M
O	S	O	M	I	O	N	E	P	L	A	A	A	A	A
S	A	L	I	S	H	H	A	H	M	N	B	G	A	J
L	R	L	U	I	U	P	N	E	A	A	G	R	T	H
S	E	O	B	K	O	E	O	N	N	M	I	R	Y	N
S	O	P	A	T	E	R	I	R	A	S	E	P	C	O
L	Q	A	Y	R	N	A	A	T	T	T	Z	H	H	E
G	U	O	Q	D	S	B	T	A	E	F	N	I	I	M
A	G	A	B	U	S	H	R	P	C	H	C	L	C	I
T	F	O	P	B	I	C	O	R	N	E	L	I	U	S
E	U	L	J	A	H	L	U	C	I	U	S	P	S	H
A	H	T	S	U	N	A	A	Y	H	T	O	M	I	T
S	X	S	S	U	P	S	I	R	C	U	I	C	U	L

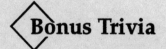

Bonus Trivia

In whose song are the words, "He hath put down the mighty from their seats, and exalted them of low degree"?

Mary's. Luke 1:52.

28
BIBLICAL DISEASES

Joe Saxton

APHASIA	GOUT
APOPLEXY	HEARING LOSS
BLAINS	LAMENESS
BLEMISHES	LEPROSY
BLINDNESS	MALARIA
BOILS	PALSY
CANCER	PLAGUE
CONSUMPTION	POLIO
DEPRESSION	RINGWORM
DYSENTERY	SMALLPOX
EDEMA	SUNSTROKE
EPILEPSY	SYNCOPE
FEVER	TUBERCULOSIS
GANGRENE	WORMS

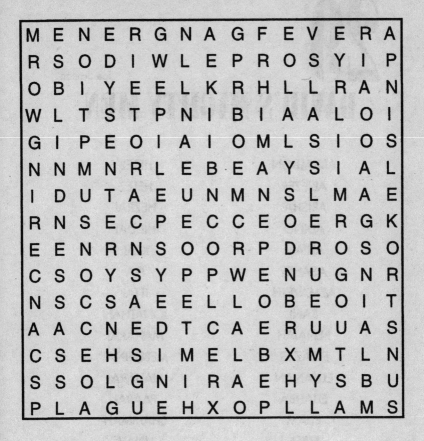

```
M E N E R G N A G F E V E R A
R S O D I W L E P R O S Y I P
O B I Y E E L K R H L L R A N
W L T S T P N I B I A A L O I
G I P E O I A I O M L S I O S
N N M N R L E B E A Y S I A L
I D U T A E U N M N S L M A E
R N S E C P E C C E O E R G K
E E N R N S O O R P D R O S O
C S O Y S Y P P W E N U G N R
N S C S A E E L L O B E O I T
A A C N E D T C A E R U U A S
C S E H S I M E L B X M T L N
S S O L G N I R A E H Y S B U
P L A G U E H X O P L L A M S
```

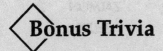

Bonus Trivia

What is Paul's saying contrasting the letter and the spirit?

"The letter killeth, but the spirit giveth life."
2 Corinthians 3:6.

29

Joe Saxton

DAVID'S MIGHTY MEN

ABI-ALBON	HELEB
ABIEZER	HELEZ
ABISHAI	HEZRAI
ADINO	HIDDAI
AHIAM	IGAL
ASAHEL	IRA
AZMAVETH	ITTAI
BANI	JONATHAN
BENAIAH	MAHARAI
ELEAZAR	MEBUNNAI
ELHANAN	NAHARAI
ELIAHBA	PAARAI
ELIAM	SHAMMAH
ELIKA	URIAH
ELIPHELET	ZALMON
GAREB	ZELEK

```
M O J R A Z E L E K P Z I A A
A U O A C E L I K A C H A D Z
I D N Z B D R H A B I E Z E R
H I A A A I W R W N R R L D A
A A T E N A A P E P N E A A X
N D H L I I D L I M H U N N T
T D A E A L I Y B A A A B H T
S I N T E A N A I O H I S E E
B H T H H N O G R A N S L L M
E I A B O D A J R A V E I E M
R S A M E L N A N A H L E B L
A R L R M H I H O P E A K A A
G A F N C A H A I R U R M Y C
Z I A R Z E H L B E N A I A H
S A M S H T E V A M Z A R E J
```

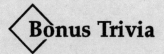

Bonus Trivia

Finish Peter's saying, "One day is with the Lord as a thousand years—."

"And a thousand years as one day."
2 Peter 3:8.

61

30

Dale Frederick Lein

WOMEN OF THE BIBLE

ABIGAIL	MICHAL
ASENATH	NAOMI
BATHSHEBA	PHOEBE
DEBORAH	PRISCILLA
DELILAH	RACHEL
DINAH	RAHAB
ELISABETH	REBEKAH
ESTHER	RHODA
EUNICE	RUTH
EVE	SALOME
JEZEBEL	SAPPHIRA
LEAH	SARAH
LOIS	TABITHA
MARTHA	TAMAR
MARY	

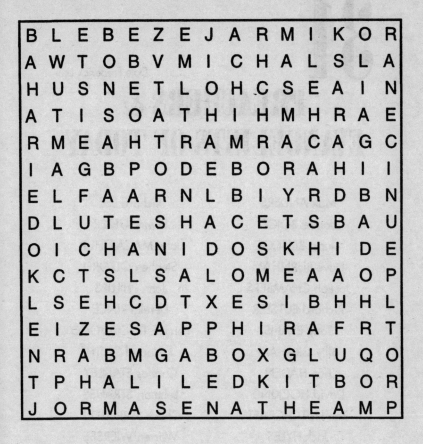

```
B L E B E Z E J A R M I K O R
A W T O B V M I C H A L S L A
H U S N E T L O H C S E A I N
A T I S O A T H I H M H R A E
R M E A H T R A M R A C A G C
I A G B P O D E B O R A H I I
E L F A A R N L B I Y R D B N
D L U T E S H A C E T S B A U
O I C H A N I D O S K H I D E
K C T S L S A L O M E A A O P
L S E H C D T X E S I B H H L
E I Z E S A P P H I R A F R T
N R A B M G A B O X G L U Q O
T P H A L I L E D K I T B O R
J O R M A S E N A T H E A M P
```

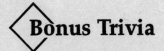

Bonus Trivia

What is the rest of the saying, "Better is it that thou shouldest not vow—."

"Than that thou shouldest vow and not pay."
Ecclesiastes 5:5.

31

Dale Frederick Lein

PREACHERS & EVANGELISTS OF TODAY

Max ANDERS

James BOICE

Stuart BRISCOE

Dave BURNHAM

Joseph CHAMBERS

Richard EUTSLER

Tony EVANS

Billy GRAHAM

Ben HADEN

David HOCKING

Ron HUTCHCRAFT

Jack HYLES

Greg LAURIE

Richard LEE

Erwin LUTZER

John MACARTHUR

Stephen OLFORD

John PHILLIPS

Derek PRINCE

Perry F. ROCKWOOD

J. Harold SMITH

Charles STANLEY

Lehman STRAUSS

Chuck SWINDOLL

Warren WIERSBE

R	E	L	G	N	I	K	C	O	H	G	M	I	D	C
A	U	P	W	E	A	D	R	E	Z	T	U	L	F	S
M	A	H	A	R	G	O	S	K	C	T	R	S	I	B
G	E	I	T	U	D	O	E	Z	F	O	E	E	W	S
O	S	L	Y	R	T	W	I	A	Q	A	L	B	M	R
E	V	L	M	O	A	K	R	U	O	H	S	I	Y	E
B	U	I	B	L	I	C	U	D	S	D	T	W	S	B
S	H	P	C	R	H	O	A	O	R	H	U	B	W	M
R	N	S	G	C	I	R	L	M	E	S	E	O	I	A
E	B	A	T	P	E	S	A	L	D	T	V	I	N	H
I	M	U	V	A	J	H	C	K	N	R	E	C	D	C
W	H	A	D	E	N	P	U	O	A	A	O	E	O	A
E	C	N	I	R	P	L	H	G	E	U	W	F	L	S
T	D	I	U	C	K	C	E	J	C	S	R	I	L	F
A	O	B	E	N	S	E	L	Y	H	S	O	B	A	O

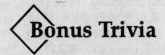

Bonus Trivia

In what Book is the great affirmation, "Hear, O Israel: The Lord our God is one Lord"?

Deuteronomy 6:4.

32

Dale Frederick Lein

PREACHERS & EVANGELISTS OF YESTERYEAR

Hyman J. APPELMAN
(1902-1983)

Donald BARNHOUSE
(1895-1960)

J. Wilbur CHAPMAN
(1859-1918)

M.R. DEHAAN (1891-1965)

A.C. DIXON (1854-1925)

Jonathan EDWARDS
(1703-1758)

Charles G. FINNEY
(1792-1875)

Arno C. GAEBELEIN
(1861-1945)

A.J. GORDON (1836-1895)

Oliver B. GREENE
(1915-1976)

H.A. IRONSIDE (1876-1951)

Clarence LARKIN (1850-1924)

R.G. LEE (1886-1978)

Martyn LLOYD-JONES
(1899-1981)

Herbert LOCKYER
(1886-1984)

Alexander MACLAREN
(1826-1910)

J. Vernon McGEE (1904-1988)

F.B. MEYER (1847-1929)

Dwight L. MOODY
(1837-1899)

G. Campbell MORGAN
(1863-1945)

John R. RICE (1895-1980)

J.C. RYLE (1816-1900)

J. Oswald SANDERS
(1902-1992)

Charles SPURGEON
(1834-1892)

Billy SUNDAY (1862-1935)

R.A. TORREY (1856-1928)

A.W. TOZER (1897-1963)

George W. TRUETT
(1867-1944)

John WESLEY (1703-1791)

George WHITEFIELD
(1714-1770)

```
W A S H G E N A M L E P P A N
H D L C T S M E Y G N M L E R
I P I R A E C S R A B O B M O
T N J X Y S G E A A C D S L S
E O C E O L E H R K L C O A G
F E R N W N E N Y D H C N I C
I G N R E D H E O O Z D A H E
E R I C E O R X L J E E A M N
L U E R U Y J T G R D P C O I
D P L S O T E N S W M Y W H K
O S E F O N O N A A D A O S R
B A B Z S D S R N O K D E L A
T T E U R T D I O I X N G O L
I R A O D S J M D T F U R N D
N A G R O M K E Y E L S E W O
```

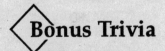

Bonus Trivia

Who asked the question, "Shall we receive good at the hand of God, and shall we not receive evil"?

Job. Job 2:10.

33

Dale Frederick Lein

NAMES AND TITLES OF JESUS CHRIST

ALPHA

CHRIST

DEITY

DELIVERER

DOOR

GOD

GREAT SHEPHERD

HIGH PRIEST

HOLY ONE

IMMANUEL

JESUS

KING OF KINGS

LAMB

LIFE

LIGHT

LION

LORD

MESSIAH

OMEGA

PRINCE OF PEACE

PROPHET

REDEEMER

ROCK

SAVIOUR

SON OF GOD

TRUE VINE

TRUTH

WAY

WORD

```
A D E L I V E R E R A H P L A
W U R C O H K N T D R O I E R
E O G E W R I F O B W F C U I
K L R A H V D G A M E A O N H
C I Y D E P F N H R E I J A A
O G N U V O E O L P V G L M I
T H R G N T L H F A R J A M S
R T A O O Y G O S E M I H I S
E E S H O F E B U T C B E U E
M H C N K C K Q E R A D S S M
E P E C N H D I A D H E D M T
E O O I S R N O N O J I R H R
D R R F M I O A O G U T O G U
E P L I T S I L E R S Y A L T
R U S N E T L O H C S I S D H
```

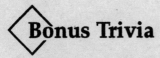

Bonus Trivia

What proverb about grapes did Ezekiel refute?

"The fathers have eaten sour grapes, and the children's teeth are set on edge."
Ezekiel 18:2.

69

34

NOAH'S FLOOD

Cathy Spies

ARK

BEASTS

BIRD

CATTLE

COMMANDED

DOVE

EARTH

FEMALE

FLOOD

FORTY

FOWLS

GOD

HAM

HEAVEN

HOUSE

JAPHETH

LIFE

MALE

NOAH

RAIN

SHEM

TWO

VIOLENCE

WATER

WOOD

```
G D F L O O D S C T R F O B A
X O P N L I O T R A G O D L R
P C D D K E V X T D T R H I K
O G N G R I E O W V I T P S I
B Z R O D P O R O B S Y L T K
C O M M A N D E D N L C R E J
W O O D M H L I S H E M K A A
A R I N W E T W D O B N S R P
T L F X M A L E N U Y T T T H
E J E H O V M L K S A I O H E
R K M U F E L I F E L H B R T
L A A X O N F R A M R A I N H
M T L V I R E V I I B M S N V
Z I E V I O L E N C E F R E O
F O W L S X D Y C B E A S T S
```

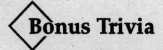

Bonus Trivia

Who did Christ say are His brother, His sister, and His mother?

35

Cathy Spies

MOSES' MISSION

AFFLICTION

BURNING

BUSH

CRY

EGYPT

FIRE

FLAME

FLOCK

GENERATION

GOLD

HONEY

ISRAEL

JEWELS

JOURNEY

LAND

LORD

MILK

MOSES

MOUNTAIN

PEOPLE

PHARAOH

SACRIFICE

SILVER

SMITE

SORROW

WILDERNESS

WONDERS

```
M K C A F F L I C T I O N K P
O O B G Z L A C R X G L H W H
S Z U E K A N F Y K E R I F A
E M S N P M D H E A B L E L R
S U H E T E T X R F D C M P A
T M U R R A R S O E I Q S R O
X O I A I C I O R F Y E N O H
S U B T B U R N I N G T V U X
R N M I E L E R Y M R S Z S W
P T Q O U S C F P E Z O N R S
M A S N S A L D V L N R W E L
O I V D S O R L R P W R O D E
U N L T C A I Q I O V O U N W
Z O X K Z S Q I F E L W X O E
G T Y B A I E G Y P T A C W J
```

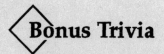

Bonus Trivia

Finish Paul's sentence, "Ye are all the children of God—."

By faith in Christ Jesus." Galatians 3:26.

73

36
PLAGUES STRIKE EGYPT

Cathy Spies

AARON	HEART
ANIMALS	HORDES
BLOOD	LAND
BOILS	LICE
DARKNESS	LIVESTOCK
DEATH	LOCUSTS
DECEITFUL	MOSES
DUST	OBEY
EGYPT	PHARAOH
FIRSTBORN	RIVER
FLIES	ROD
FROGS	SERPENT
HAIL	SICK
HAND	SWARMS

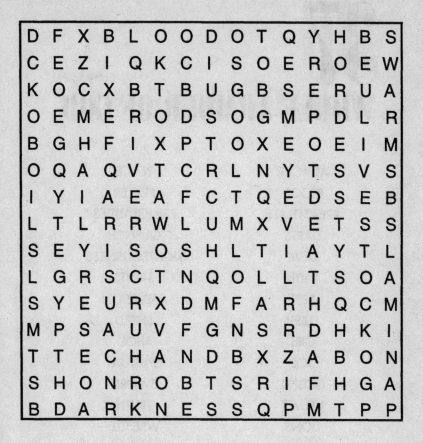

```
D F X B L O O D O T Q Y H B S
C E Z I Q K C I S O E R O E W
K O C X B T B U G B S E R U A
O E M E R O D S O G M P D L R
B G H F I X P T O X E O E I M
O Q A Q V T C R L N Y T S V S
I Y I A E A F C T Q E D S E B
L T L R R W L U M X V E T S S
S E Y I S O S H L T I A Y T L
L G R S C T N Q O L L T S O A
S Y E U R X D M F A R H Q C M
M P S A U V F G N S R D H K I
T T E C H A N D B X Z A B O N
S H O N R O B T S R I F H G A
B D A R K N E S S Q P M T P P
```

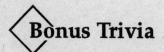

Bonus Trivia

Give the sentence from the Revelation which ends, "and their works do follow them."

"Blessed are the dead which die in the Lord from henceforth: Yea, saith the Spirit, that they may rest from their labours; and their works do follow them." Revelation 14:13.

37
WHOLE ARMOUR OF GOD

Cathy Spies

ARMOUR	PEACE
BLOOD	PRAYER
BREASTPLATE	PRINCIPALITIES
DARTS	QUENCH
DEVIL	RIGHTEOUSNESS
FAITH	SAINTS
FEET	SALVATION
FLESH	SHIELD
GIRT	SHOD
GOD	SPIRITUAL
GOSPEL	SWORD
HELMET	TRUTH
LIONS	WRESTLE

```
H S E L F U D E V I L V G O D
S A L V A T I O N W S I T S B
E I M X O L A U T I R I P S G
I N D A R T S O R T B L M E C
T T H F E E T T E R N E V N E
I S J A M T K E Y P Q P U S Q
L A E I F K A M A Z X S H U U
A F L T C E R L R S T O V O E
P G T H O X M E P W D G Z E N
I V S R T V O H X T N O L T C
C L E H U W U L D S S G X H H
N I R D I T R Q F W N A F G B
I M W F S E H B O A C O E I Q
R Q H B Z R L R S B Q T I R E
P E A C E X D D U M D O O L B
```

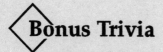 **Bonus Trivia**

To what does the proverb compare pleasant words?

"Pleasant words are as an honeycomb, sweet to the soul, and health to the bones."
Proverbs 16:24.

38
BOOKS OF THE BIBLE: PART 1

Cathy Spies

GENESIS	NEHEMIAH
EXODUS	ESTHER
LEVITICUS	JOB
NUMBERS	PSALMS
DEUTERONOMY	PROVERBS
JOSHUA	ECCLESIASTES
JUDGES	(SONG OF) SOLOMON
RUTH	ISAIAH
SAMUEL	JEREMIAH
KINGS	LAMENTATIONS
CHRONICLES	EZEKIEL
EZRA	DANIEL

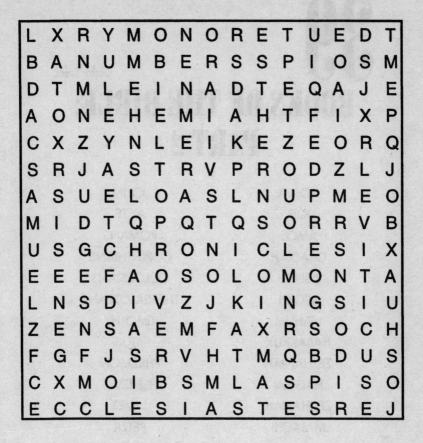

```
L X R Y M O N O R E T U E D T
B A N U M B E R S S P I O S M
D T M L E I N A D T E Q A J E
A O N E H E M I A H T F I X P
C X Z Y N L E I K E Z E O R Q
S R J A S T R V P R O D Z L J
A S U E L O A S L N U P M E O
M I D T Q P Q T S O R R V B
U S G C H R O N I C L E S I X
E E E F A O S O L O M O N T A
L N S D I V Z J K I N G S I U
Z E N S A E M F A X R S O C H
F G F J S R V H T M Q B D U S
C X M O I B S M L A S P I S O
E C C L E S I A S T E S R E J
```

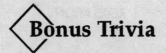

Bonus Trivia

Finish the words of the psalm, "My soul,
wait thou only upon God; for—."

"My expectation is from him." Psalms 62:5.

79

39

Cathy Spies

BOOKS OF THE BIBLE: PART 2

HOSEA	JOHN
JOEL	ACTS
AMOS	ROMANS
OBADIAH	CORINTHIANS
JONAH	COLOSSIANS
MICAH	THESSALONIANS
NAHUM	TIMOTHY
HABAKKUK	TITUS
ZEPHANIAH	PHILEMON
HAGGAI	HEBREWS
ZECHARIAH	JAMES
MALACHI	PETER
MATTHEW	JUDE
MARK	REVELATION
LUKE	

```
T I M O T H Y I C P E T E R Z
Q H Z M P H I L E M O N C E E
P E E X L K Y D J A M E S V C
I B P S B L J X O B A D I A H
H R H N S O I O H R C K X N A
C E A B E A Q L N O R L M O R
A W N L G E L K L A N E S I I
L S I G U I U O M Q H D N T A
A Y A O N K S W N K E U A A H
M H H S K S E N E I L J M L B
I Z T A I P A K Q H A T O E Y
C C B A S M E P M X T N R V Z
A A N X O Y S S U T I T S E T
H S R S T Z O L X Y B O A R R
C O R I N T H I A N S I E M S
```

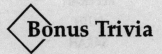 **Bonus Trivia**

To whom was it said, "Dust thou art, and unto dust shalt thou return"?

To Adam, by God. Genesis 3:19.

40
WOMEN IN THE BIBLE

Teresa Zook

ABIGAIL	LEAH
ABITAL	LOIS
ACHSAH	LYDIA
AHINOAM	MAACHAH
ANNA	MARTHA
BATHSHEBA	MICHAL
BATHSHUA	MIRIAM
CANDACE	NAARAH
DEBORAH	NAOMI
DORCAS	ORPAH
EGLAH	PHOEBE
ELIZABETH	PRISCILLA
ESTHER	RACHEL
EUNICE	RAHAB
EVE	REBEKAH
HAGGITH	RUTH
HANNAH	SARAH
HELAH	TABITHA
HERODIAS	TAMAR
JEZEBEL	

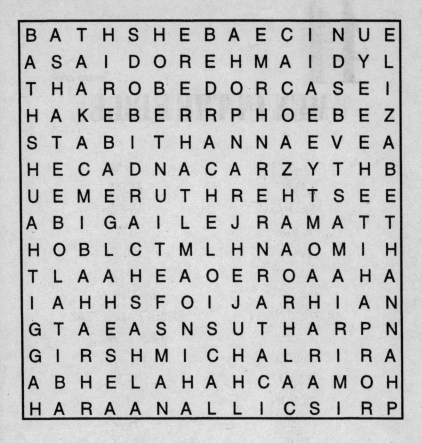

```
B A T H S H E B A E C I N U E
A S A I D O R E H M A I D Y L
T H A R O B E D O R C A S E I
H A K E B E R R P H O E B E Z
S T A B I T H A N N A E V E A
H E C A D N A C A R Z Y T H B
U E M E R U T H R E H T S E E
A B I G A I L E J R A M A T T
H O B L C T M L H N A O M I H
T L A A H E A O E R O A A H A
I A H H S F O I J A R H I A N
G T A E A S N S U T H A R P N
G I R S H M I C H A L R I R A
A B H E L A H A H C A A M O H
H A R A A N A L L I C S I R P
```

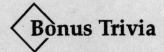

Bonus Trivia

Complete the war cry, "The sword of the Lord—."

"And of Gideon." Judges 7:18.

41

Teresa Zook

MEN IN THE BIBLE

AARON	JOSHUA
ABEL	JUDAS
ABRAHAM	LAMECH
ADAM	LOT
AHAB	LUKE
AMOS	MARK
ANDREW	MATTHEW
BARTHOLOMEW	NEBUCHADNEZZAR
CALEB	NICODEMUS
DAVID	NOAH
ESAU	PAUL
GIDEON	PETER
HOSEA	PHILIP
HUR	PILATE
ISAAC	SAMUEL
JACOB	SAUL
JAMES	SIMON
JEHOSHAPHAT	SOLOMON
JOHN	TERAH
JONAH	THADDEUS
JONATHAN	THOMAS

```
J O N A T H A N W E H T T A M
A E J O S H U A M A H A R B A
M S H E T A L I P O M A R K W
E A N O A H N O M O L O S E W
S U J E S S S A M U E L M T E
I S A A C H S L E B A O E H R
M R H O S E A H A B L R J A D
O U D A V I D P U O A M O D N
N H O J U D A S H H S A N D A
O P N A M O S T T A C D A E P
E E O C H R R O I S T A H U A
D T R O C A L E B T L U A S U
I E A B B L A M E C H E K U L
G R A Z Z E N D A H C U B E N
N I C O D E M U S P H I L I P
```

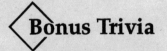

Bonus Trivia

Who said, "We will give ourselves continually to prayer, and to the ministry of the word"?

85

42

Teresa Zook

CITIES IN PALESTINE

ANTIPATRIS	HERODIUM
ARIMATHEA	JERICHO
ASHKELON	JERUSALEM
BETHANY	JOPPA
BETHLEHEM	LYDDA
BETHSAIDA	MAGDALA
CAESAREA	NAIN
CANA	NAZARETH
CAPERNAUM	SAMARIA
EMMAUS	SIDON
EPHRAIM	SYCHAR
GAZA	TYRE
GERASA	
HEBRON	

```
C A D I A S H T E B A P P O J
B A A C E I E H S I D O N E K
E B E F D G B J N A I N R H L
T M A S N T R O R T M I A T C
H E E U A Y O Q P S C R L E A
L L H V W R N B X H L A A R N
E A T A Z E E Y O C Y H D A A
H S A B E T H A N Y D C G Z D
E U M E A S A R E G D Y A A F
M R I G Z A I R A M A S M N H
I E R J A S I R T A P I T N A
M J A L G C A P E R N A U M K
N E P H R A I M O S U A M M E
A S H K E L O N A E J I D Q P
H L F B H E R O D I U M C G K
```

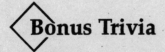

Bonus Trivia

Who said of marriage, "What therefore God hath joined together, let not man put asunder"?

Christ. Mark 10:9.

43

Teresa Zook

BOOKS OF THE NEW TESTAMENT

MATTHEW

MARK

LUKE

JOHN

ACTS

ROMANS

CORINTHIANS

GALATIANS

EPHESIANS

PHILIPPIANS

COLOSSIANS

THESSALONIANS

TIMOTHY

TITUS

PHILEMON

HEBREWS

JAMES

PETER

FIRST JOHN

SECOND JOHN

THIRD JOHN

JUDE

REVELATION

```
C C A B C M A T T H E W D Z E
F O T H E S S A L O N I A N S
G L R H S N A I P P I L I H P
I O F I R E V E L A T I O N J
K S I P N L O Q S V S M U X P
A S R H B T C E D U J E K U L
S I S I N Y H D T R E P W N Y
T A T L F H G I T H I H J H K
C N J E L T T M A N P E H O O
A S O M Q O R T S N U S E J S
S V H O X M A R K Y S I B D N
E A N N W I C G K E I A R R A
M D H R E T E P J L Z N E I M
A O N H O J D N O C E S W H O
J B H F G A L A T I A N S T R
```

Bonus Trivia

Finish the verse of the psalm, "O thou that hearest prayer—."

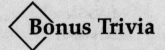

"Unto thee shall all flesh come." Psalms 65:2.

44

Teresa Zook

BOOKS OF THE OLD TESTAMENT

GENESIS	SONG OF SOLOMON
EXODUS	ISAIAH
LEVITICUS	JEREMIAH
NUMBERS	LAMENTATIONS
DEUTERONOMY	EZEKIEL
JOSHUA	DANIEL
JUDGES	JOEL
RUTH	AMOS
SAMUEL	OBADIAH
KINGS	JONAH
CHRONICLES	NAHUM
EZRA	HABAKKUK
NEHEMIAH	ZEPHANIAH
ESTHER	HAGGAI
JOB	ZECHARIAH
PSALMS	MALACHI
ECCLESIASTES	

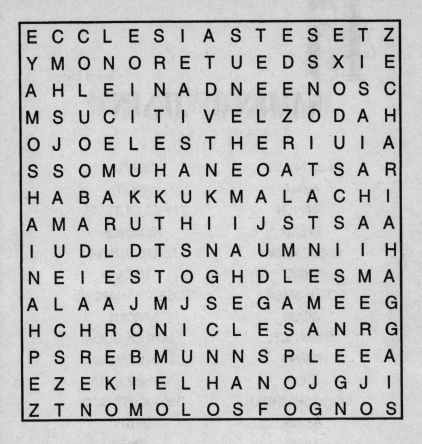

```
E C C L E S I A S T E S E T Z
Y M O N O R E T U E D S X I E
A H L E I N A D N E E N O S C
M S U C I T I V E L Z O D A H
O J O E L E S T H E R I U I A
S S O M U H A N E O A T S A R
H A B A K K U K M A L A C H I
A M A R U T H I I J S T S A A
I U D L D T S N A U M N I I H
N E I E S T O G H D L E S M A
A L A A J M J S E G A M E E G
H C H R O N I C L E S A N R G
P S R E B M U N N S P L E E A
E Z E K I E L H A N O J G J I
Z T N O M O L O S F O G N O S
```

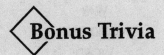

Bonus Trivia

Who said, "I am doing a great work, so that I cannot come down"?

Nehemiah. Nehemiah 6:3.

45

Teresa Zook

NAMES OF JESUS

ALL (IN ALL)   OMEGA

ALPHA   PRIEST

BRANCH   PRINCE OF PEACE

BREAD   REDEEMER

BRIDEGROOM   RESURRECTION

CHRIST   ROCK

COUNSELOR   ROSE (OF SHARON)

DOOR   SAVIOUR

EMMANUEL   SON OF GOD

FRIEND   SON OF MAN

GOD   (MORNING) STAR

GOOD SHEPHERD   THE MIGHTY GOD

JESUS   TRUTH

LAMB   VINE

LIFE   WAY

LIGHT   WONDERFUL

LORD OF LORDS   WORD

MESSIAH   (LIVING) WATER

```
T K H L O R D O F L O R D S N
H B C I S R O L E S N U O C A
E R N G I U A H P L A W M N M
M I A H G O S L I F E O E N F
I D R T R E D E E M E R G O O
G E B W A T E R J F K D A I N
H G O O D S H E P H E R D T O
T R L U F R E D N O W T A C S
Y O E D N E I R F W E R E E A
G O U P R I E S T A S U R R V
O M N D O O R S I Y O T B R I
D R A N G V I K C O R H G U O
L A M B I R D O G F O N O S U
L T M N H A I S S E M S D E R
A S E C A E P F O E C N I R P
```

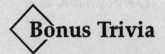

Bonus Trivia

Finish the proverb, "Trust in the Lord with all thy heart; and—."

"Lean not unto thine own understanding." Proverbs 3:5.

46

William Johns

JOSEPH

ASENATH	JACOB
BAKER	KINE
BASKETS	MIDIANITES
BUTLER	MONEY
CAMELS	MOON
COAT	NUTS
CUP	PIT
DIE	POTI-PHERAH
DOTHAN	PRISON
DREAMER	RACHEL
EGYPT	SHEAVES
EMBALM	SHECHEM
FORGIVE	SUN
FORTY	VINE
GOSHEN	ZAPHNATH-PAANEAH
HEBREW	

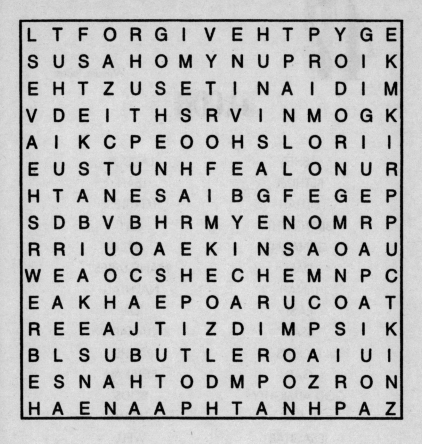

```
L T F O R G I V E H T P Y G E
S U S A H O M Y N U P R O I K
E H T Z U S E T I N A I D I M
V D E I T H S R V I N M O G K
A I K C P E O O H S L O R I I
E U S T U N H F E A L O N U R
H T A N E S A I B G F E G E P
S D B V B H R M Y E N O M R P
R R I U O A E K I N S A O A U
W E A O C S H E C H E M N P C
E A K H A E P O A R U C O A T
R E E A J T I Z D I M P S I K
B L S U B U T L E R O A I U I
E S N A H T O D M P O Z R O N
H A E N A A P H T A N H P A Z
```

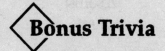

Bonus Trivia

To what did Paul compare the coming of "the day of the Lord"?

"As a thief in the night." 1 Thessolians 5:2.

47

William Johns

JACOB

ASHER	LADDER
BETHUEL	LEAH
BILHAH	LENTILES
BIRTHRIGHT	LEVI
CANAAN	LUZ
DAN	MANDRAKES
DINAH	NAPHTALI
EAST	OIL
ESAU	PADANARAM
FLOCKS	RACHEL
GAD	REBEKAH
GOD ALMIGHTY	RODS
ISAAC	VOW
ISSACHAR	WELL
JOSEPH	ZEBULUN
LABAN	ZILPAH

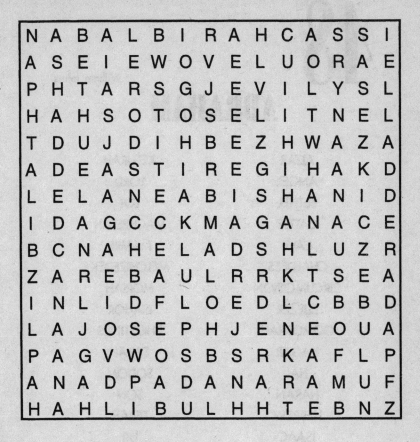

```
N A B A L B I R A H C A S S I
A S E I E W O V E L U O R A E
P H T A R S G J E V I L Y S L
H A H S O T O S E L I T N E L
T D U J D I H B E Z H W A Z A
A D E A S T I R E G I H A K D
L E L A N E A B I S H A N I D
I D A G C C K M A G A N A C E
B C N A H E L A D S H L U Z R
Z A R E B A U L R R K T S E A
I N L I D F L O E D L C B B D
L A J O S E P H J E N E O U A
P A G V W O S B S R K A F L P
A N A D P A D A N A R A M U F
H A H L I B U L H H T E B N Z
```

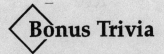

Bonus Trivia

Of whom is it said in Hebrews that of them
"the world was not worthy"?

The Old Testament men and women of faith.
Hebrews 11:38.

48

William Johns

ABRAHAM

ALTAR	KETURAH
ANGEL	LORD
BETHEL	LOT
CATTLE	MACHPELAH
CAVE	MAMRE
CHALDEES	MELCHIZEDEK
CIRCUMCISION	MORIAH
ELIEZER	NAHOR
GOMORRAH	PHILISTINES
HAGAR	SARAH
HAI	SODOM
HARAN	SON
HEBREW	TERAH
ISAAC	UR
ISHMAEL	ZOAR

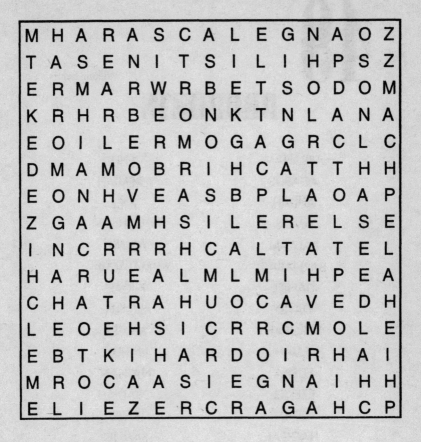

```
M H A R A S C A L E G N A O Z
T A S E N I T S I L I H P S Z
E R M A R W R B E T S O D O M
K R H R B E O N K T N L A N A
E O I L E R M O G A G R C L C
D M A M O B R I H C A T T H H
E O N H V E A S B P L A O A P
Z G A A M H S I L E R E L S E
I N C R R R H C A L T A T E L
H A R U E A L M L M I H P E A
C H A T R A H U O C A V E D H
L E O E H S I C R R C M O L E
E B T K I H A R D O I R H A I
M R O C A A S I E G N A I H H
E L I E Z E R C R A G A H C P
```

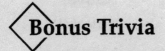

Bonus Trivia

What is the saying in Hosea about being "joined to idols"?

"Ephraim is joined to idols: let him alone."
Hosea 4:17.

49

William Johns

PROPHETS

ABRAHAM	JEHU
AGABUS	JEREMIAH
AHIJAH	JOEL
AMOS	JOHN
BALAAM	JONAH
BARNABAS	MALACHI
DANIEL	MICAH
DAVID	MICAIAH
DEBORAH	MOSES
ELIJAH	NAHUM
ELISHA	NATHAN
EZEKIEL	OBADIAH
GAD	PAUL
HAGGAI	SAMUEL
HOSEA	SIMEON
ISAIAH	ZEPHANIAH

```
L S A B A N R A B A D L S O H
E I H B E D H S U H E J H A J
I M S U R I F U Z U H O I K O
K E U A J O H B M B C M J M H
E O P A I M U A G A E O O A N
Z N H K P A S G M R Z S N M A
E I A G G A H A E N E Z A U T
D A N I E L H J D S C O H H H
O B A D I A H O M I C A H A A
A S I M R B G C L P V P I N N
H D E B O R A H E E E A L A B
S I A S I S A I O Z C U D A G
I S A E S O H A J I L E G O A
L U A P B A L A M A L A C H I
E F H A I N A H P E Z G I N S
```

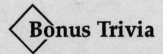

Bonus Trivia

What command follows "Cease to do evil"?

"Learn to do well." Isaiah 1:16,17.

101

50

William Johns

CHRIST'S PASSION

ANNAS	KINGDOM
BARABBAS	LANTERNS
BETRAYED	LAW
CAIAPHAS	LINEN
CEDRON	MALCHUS
CHIEF PRIESTS	OFFICERS
COCK	PHARISEES
CROWN	PURPLE
CRUCIFY	SCOURGED
CUP	SIMON
DAMSEL	SOLDIERS
DISCIPLES	SON
JEWS	SYNAGOGUE
JUDAS	TEMPLE
JUDGMENT HALL	TORCHES

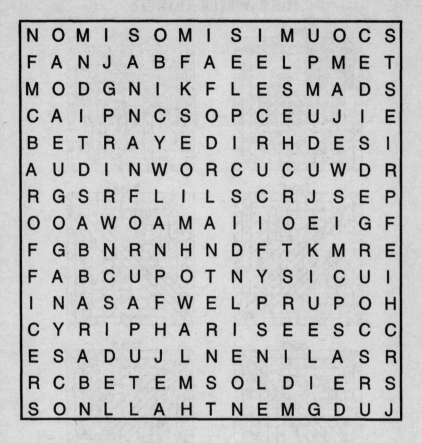

```
N O M I S O M I S I M U O C S
F A N J A B F A E E L P M E T
M O D G N I K F L E S M A D S
C A I P N C S O P C E U J I E
B E T R A Y E D I R H D E S I
A U D I N W O R C U C U W D R
R G S R F L I L S C R J S E P
O O A W O A M A I I O E I G F
F G B N R N H N D F T K M R E
F A B C U P O T N Y S I C U I
I N A S A F W E L P R U P O H
C Y R I P H A R I S E E S C C
E S A D U J L N E N I L A S R
R C B E T E M S O L D I E R S
S O N L L A H T N E M G D U J
```

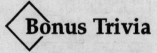

Bonus Trivia

What is Christ's saying about the coming night?

"The night cometh, when no man can work."
John 9:4.

Word Search Answers

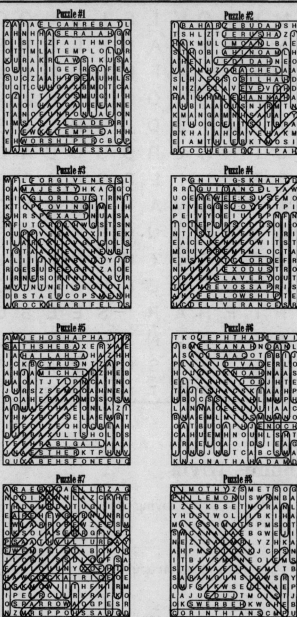

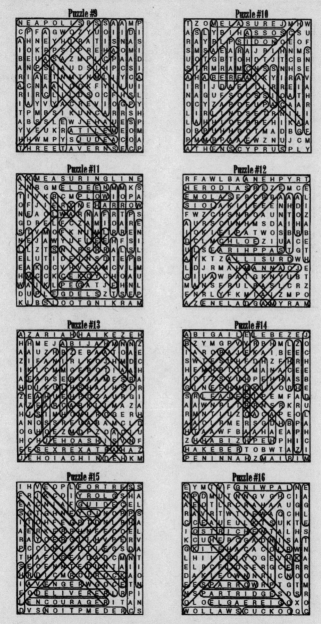

105

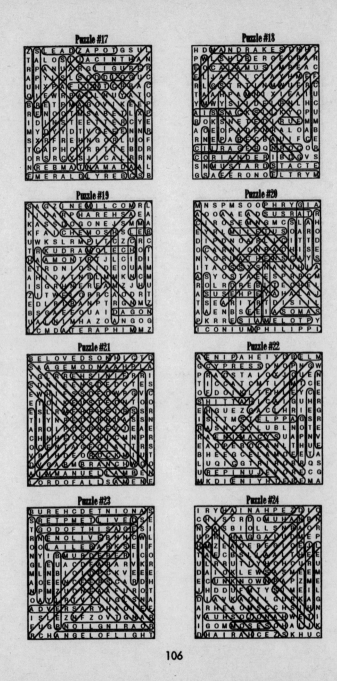

Puzzle #17

Puzzle #18

Puzzle #19

Puzzle #20

Puzzle #21

Puzzle #22

Puzzle #23

Puzzle #24

106

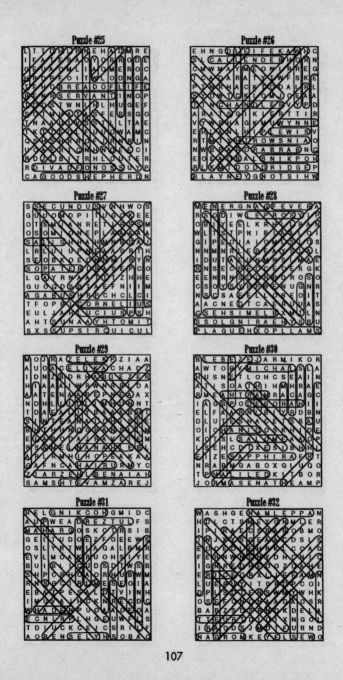

Puzzle #25

Puzzle #26

Puzzle #27

Puzzle #28

Puzzle #29

Puzzle #30

Puzzle #31

Puzzle #32

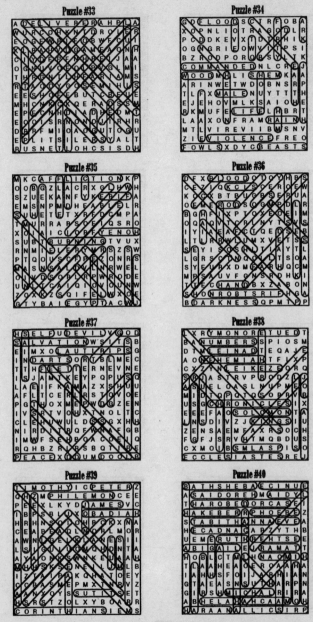

108

Puzzle #41

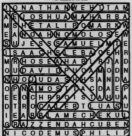

Puzzle #42

Puzzle #43

Puzzle #44

Puzzle #45

Puzzle #46

Puzzle #47

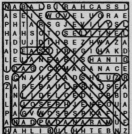

Puzzle #48

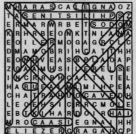

Puzzle #49

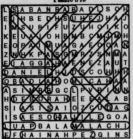

Puzzle #50

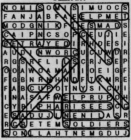

110